T0208043

Letters in the Lunchbag

ARNO ILIC

LETTERS IN THE LUNCHBAG

iUniverse books may be ordered through booksellers or by contacting:

iUniverse
1663 Liberty Drive
Bloomington, IN 47403
www.iuniverse.com
1-800-Authors (1-800-288-4677)

ISBN: 978-1-5320-6131-8 (sc)
ISBN: 978-1-5320-6132-5 (e)

Print information available on the last page.

iUniverse rev. date: 01/092019

To Norma

Introduction

It started simply enough. My wife would include little notes with my lunch from time to time. When I read the notes, I felt just a little more connected to her and the fact that she wrote the notes indicated to me that she loved me; for she took the time to add the little notes into my lunch.

After some years, I found myself out of work, so I had time to prepare her lunch. I thought it might be a good idea to add a note to her lunch to express my feelings for her, and to give her something to read while enjoying her lunch. These are some of the notes that I kept. I decided to put them into a book to share with my wife, family and friends. I not only wanted my wife to know how I felt about her, but all those that have contributed to our family and know us.

In some of the notes you will find a reference to "Ashie". It is a nickname that I gave Norma all these years ago, long before we were married. I also refer to her as FP or Fairy Princess. When I was looking for a companion, I always had in mind that I wanted my own Fairy Princess, just like in the story books. If I found her, I knew that I would live happily after.

Norma is my Fairy Princess, and from the day I first laid eyes on her and told myself that this is the one, until today, she has continued to make this marriage a happy one. Of course, you can't have a Fairy Princess without a Prince Charming, referred herein as PC, your faithful writer.

In some letters you will find a reference to loving you more than all the leaves on all the trees. This was an expression Norma first used with me. I got the vastness of that love, so you will find me referring to it in some of the letters.

When she tells me that her friends consider her lucky to be married to me, I smile and think that they have the entire thing reversed. No one really knows what people are like unless they live with them. Socializing with people only provides one with a singular view. Usually under those circumstances, there are no stresses. Socializing is usually when people are on their best behaviour. It is when people are under stress that you have a much better perspective of how the person really is. This is why I consider myself lucky and blessed to have Norma as my Guardian Angel and Fairy Princess.

Acknowledgements

First and foremost, I wish to thank my wife of 35 years, Norma. Without her, I would not have written this book. Her support of me over the years has been astounding. When I think of the things she has had to put up with over the years, and endured my growing pains, a lesser person would have left a long time ago. She has been a true angel, sent from wherever they come from.

My children, all five of them, one mine, two Norma's and two of ours, have always been a source of inspiration. I have learned more about leadership from them than I have in many other places. It is because of them that I try to lead by example in all that I do. Sometimes I fail, but I always try to clean it up. I found that as a father, I didn't always have to be right.

Of course I must acknowledge those that helped with the editing and graphics, my good friends Sylvan and Mona.

Sukhjit Singh, author of "Same Shoes, Different Doors" was a valuable resource for pointing me in the right direction getting this book published

There are too many people that have come into my life and contributed to mention them here. I do not wish to risk missing someone and there are numerous people that have made off-handed comments that have made a difference in my life, and they will never know it, as I have never seen them again to thank them. So to all that read this book, thank you for enriching my life.

You are the apple of my eye. You are the sunshine of my life. You make my heart flutter. You are none of those silly emails that people send depicting women as less than who they really are. You are the one I love and long to be with every moment of every day. Love, A

Sometimes we are in the house together and we each do our own thing; you on the computer, me reading. Sometimes I watch sports while you are reading or catching up with friends and family on the phone. I am always grateful that we are together as one, doing these different tasks or enjoining different interests. When the love is as strong and as wonderful as ours, there is always time to talk, to love and just to be. We don't require each of us to be different than we are. That's why I love you so much. A

Whenever I write these notes, I am automatically reminded how much I love you. The fact that I write one every day, expressing my love for you is a reminder of how grateful I am to have asked you to join me at a seminar I was attending. That single event changed my life forever and much for the better. You are a special lady and I'm glad you decided to share your life with me. Love, A.

When I look at you, all I see is a beautiful woman. Over the years we all change our appearance. We get older; add a few more wrinkles and, those really do not define us. We hear about inner beauty and indeed it is so. You take your beauty to another level. You radiate it from every pour in your body. No wonder you still carry a youthful body. Love, A

Thank you for a beautiful weekend. Eating on the deck beside the pool together has been a rare and wonderful experience, mostly due to the weather. Then there is the pleasant visit with Adam and Natasha. A nice leisurely lunch on the patio in Gravenhurst before heading home. Even though we were late getting back, it was worth it. Love, A. xoxo

I really appreciate your touch — especially when I am not well. While your concern for my well-being is touching, you don't have to worry as I am not planning on leaving this planet anytime soon. After 33 years of marriage, I still plan on growing old with you. Some may think we are already old, but we certainly don't act our age. I guess that is the thing about love — it keeps us young. Love P.C.

One of my favourite times of the day is to just sit with you and watch television. Many times I sit next to you, holding your hand and I think how lucky I have been to have you. Years ago, in my early 30s, a man said he was going to meet his Fairy Princess. How fortuitous it was to find a lady who had "Princess" in her middle name. You really are my Fairy Princess. Love, A (PC)

Ashie, as you are not going today, you will most likely be eating lunch here. Back pain takes a long while to heal. Please be careful and leave the housework to me. I love you more than all the trees and leaves. Pretty soon I will love you more than all the snowflakes on the ground. Love A.

Sometimes you can think of nothing to write. My mind agrees and even justifies it by whispering to me, "It's okay — nobody expects you to write a love note each day". Then I shift my thoughts to you and it all comes flowing back; seeing you in pyjamas, reading a book, watching television, just stepping out of the shower, giving our children advice; then it all comes rushing back on how much I really love you. A

I am a little worried about your health these days. As difficult as it is for you to handle, it becomes difficult for me too. There is this helpless feeling of not being able to do anything but watch you suffer. I wish I had a magic wand to make you feel better. I never understood why we had to pledge being with someone through sickness and in health. If you really love someone, you shouldn't have to put it in a vow. Comforting the sick is a no-brainer when it comes to you; you are a very special lady. I love you. A

You are the glue that keeps the family together. Thank you for arranging everything with the kids. Thank you for preparing the garbage too. It saved a lot of time this morning. Well, this is a short note because I am off to drop the kids to the airport. Love, PC

I can't tell you how fortunate I am to have you. It is my firm belief now that the only reason I came to Eaton's was to meet you. It was only one and one half years that I stayed and that was because it took a year to find you. I still remember my trepidation in asking you out. I don't know to this day why I was so fearful. After all, I was only asking you to join me at a seminar. Ahh, when you said yes, it was like my first date; I was elated. Of course, you actually thought it was going to be a date and were disappointed to find out it was only a seminar. Love, A.

Sometimes I think of the past and how we met. I think about how I felt about you that first day we met, the first kiss, the first love making, and then I look at you today and I see how I feel. It is not much different, but know that our love is so much deeper and having our children as an expression of that love is special. Seeing how the kids turned out and being an expression of our best has me loving you even more. God, I do love you. A

Thank you for being such a wonderful friend. I enjoyed being at the concert with you last night. It is always special holding hands and listening to great music. Enjoy this evening with the "girls". You deserve it as much as Jayne. Love, A

I love you so much that sometimes I feel I would burst.
I could just hug you all the time. You are so squeezable.
I just want to shower you with kisses; sometimes it is
nice just to be and talk work, the kids, the family or just
speculating on where we will take our next trip. Other
times, having our own space and knowing you are in the
same house is enough. Love A.

It can be somewhat disappointing to find you on the far
side of the bed when I come in later than you. I always
like to hug up to you but you are so far on the other side,
it is not possible to reach you unless I move sideways,
as your feet are on one side of the bed, and your head
on the other side. Besides, I don't wish to disturb your
sleep. When the reverse is true, I really do miss those
hugs from you. I thought I do not like you waking me
up by trying to pull me over to you but I feel much better
when I am near you, even if it means interrupting my
sleep. I actually miss the hugs. Love, A

At times the morning can be a bit of a frenzy. What's good to remember is that things pass as all other things in life. Things can go crazy at times and we can easily get caught up in it. When we take a step back, we see the path a little more clearly. So my dear, now that things are back to normal hopefully your day will run more smoothly. Love, A

I love the expression you coined for this family — huggy buggy. It became a special meaning for me. Hugs are for family and friends. Huggy buggies are just for us. It is more than a hug. A kiss is included and sometimes roaming hands are also involved. Sometimes it is just holding you with that closeness that can only come from years of living with you. Most of all, huggy buggies remind me of cozying up in bed after a long day and warming each other up, especially those could autumn and winter days. A

You send chills up and down my spine — of course they are good chills (and goose bumps too), when you come up from behind me and hug and kiss me. It reminds me of how special you are and how lucky I am to have you in my life. After 32 years of marriage, the fact that you can still do that to me is a testament or our relationship, Love, A.

As always, I really cherish our time together, especially on the weekends. Lately we have not had too many and may not for another while. It doesn't matter if we go shopping at Costco's or enjoying an evening holding hands in front of the television. It is also nice to just sit and talk in the kitchen while having supper and a glass of wine, or breakfast and coffee, discussing the previous day's events. It is really easy to love you. A

What a wonderful weekend. Friday we saw Les Miserables with your two brothers and wives, followed by coffee and dessert. Saturday we had the newlyweds over for supper and a relaxing evening, and Sunday we had your third brother over for breakfast. Then the rest of the day was ours. It actually was a perfect weekend. This morning there is snow on the ground and Christmas music on the radio. It feels more like mid-December than the middle of November. Oh well, all is great because I have you in my life. I love you lots. A

I think of you in the shower cleaning your body and me
with my dirty mind. You appeal to me just as much now
as all those years ago. We may have aged physically
but mentally we have not. We still enjoy each other's
company and can still act as though on our first date
— okay maybe the third date. Basically I still can't get
enough of you. Love, your PC

Snuggling up to you always makes me realize that we
really are one being inside two bodies. Together we have
created the world view that we live in. When I look
around all I see is love. It is what I focus on and that
is what has expanded in our life. The love we have for
one another propels us to see love all around us. Your
friends and mine reflect that back to us. It makes them
special as well as you. They become an expression of who
we are. I learned to love myself through you. Love, A

I don't often thank you for the little things you do to
make my life easier. I appreciate the fact that you get
the garbage bags ready for me. I appreciate how you
tidy up after breakfast when I regularly make a mess. I
appreciate you making the bed each morning; but most of
all I appreciate the hugs you give me each day. They all
add up to a wonderful woman. Love, A

We have people come into our lives at various times. Some just pass through, leaving us richer; some remain with us for longer and then there are those that we are fortunate to have for a lifetime. You are such a person. You continue to make a difference in my life. Some complain about how different their partners are. I celebrate our differences. You provide me with a variant view and that allows me to be a better person in the end. I love and celebrate the contrasts in our relationship. Love, A

When you came to sit beside me this morning I was a bit bewildered as I like sitting opposite you so I can see you and look into your eyes. The closeness of you sitting beside me had an electric effect that could energize a light bulb. It just goes to show, after all these years, you still stir those feelings that make my heart swell. I love you to bits and every single bit inside the bits. Love, A

Some mornings can be a bit hectic, especially when I get up late. It is always nice to be able to snuggle up in the morning. The bed is nice and warm, you have a sleepy smell about you and the rest of the house is still cold. But as hectic as things might be sometimes I always seem to find enough time to write you a little love note to say how much you mean to me. I love you so much. A

Every time I think of you, I think of those wonderful eyes of yours, that beautiful body that has held up over all those years and most of all, your tolerance and ability to forgive not only others but also my transgressions. It puts me to thinking that with your magnitude of compassion and understanding of others; I just imagine how much compassion and forgiveness God must have. You are the best thing by far that has happened in my life. Love, A

I love that we hug and kiss every morning before leaving for work because I always leave before you when many times you are just getting out of the shower. It makes hugging and kissing even more special. What a wonderful way to start a day. Thank you for being such a loving person. It makes loving you so easy. Have wonderful day. Love PC

I always look forward to the weekend. The next two should be special. I love going to concerts with you and the Christmas concert tomorrow should be special. Then, let's not forget Patrick's soirée on Sunday. While the weekend will be packed full of good stuff, the best part will be spending it with you. I love you dearly; xoxoxo, A or PC

I look at you each morning while you are doing your leg scissor lifts and I must admit to some lascivious thoughts going through my head. I hate to interrupt your exercising but the thought of taking you right there on the floor has entered my mind more than once. It is not just physical though, it's more than that; it is also your inner beauty that also has me wanting you. Your beauty simply shines through everything. You generate such high energy, it is simply amazing. I love you lots. Still charming --- Prince, that is. Love, A

I love the mornings. I get up an hour earlier than you. When I pick up the paper and wash the dishes, I am feeling a little chilly. By then it is time to wake you up. You still have that warmth of sleep about you. The desire is to crawl back into bed and start stroking you. The only problem is my hands are so cold it would be like getting an electrical shock. I love you far too much to do such a thing to you. I do love you so much, it is difficult to articulate those feelings fully. Love, PC.

When I looked at you last night, I see the same woman that I married. Since we have gone through so much together in life, we have become much wiser. We no longer worry about our insecurities as we have outgrown

them. We no longer have to defend our positions of who's right, nor do we need to impress each other. We are in a state of being-ness. There is nothing else going on than just to love one another for being exactly who we are. There is nothing to fix. Love, PC

Sometimes I wonder what to write about and then I think of you. The way you smile, the way you never talk down to people, the way your friends always feel better about themselves after having spent time with you. I love that cute turned up nose of yours, the way you do your hair and the way you look when you sleep. So when I think of what to write in your little lunch note, all I have to do is think about you. We have grown in so many ways, ways that I had hoped for and here we are. We complement each other. I love you so much. A

Okay, so yesterday I confused Thursday with being Friday, so today really is, and I am still looking forward to the weekend. And, it of course, does not change the way I feel about you. I love holding you in my arms and kissing the back of your neck. I love lying in bed knowing you are beside me. I love holding you and the passionate kisses you give me before heading out to work. Love, A.

Every morning I look at you and am reminded how much I love you. Those oversized t-shirts from Hawaii that you wear at night and early in the mornings before getting dressed just make looking at you cuter than you already are. Thank you for allowing me to share in your journey through life. Love A.

My, my, another week gone. It was wonderful. It was great to try so many different vintages of wine. William sure has quite the collection. He seems to know all the vintages and the vineyards they came from as well. For that matter, so does Bernard. Colm Wilkinson was also wonderful. Getting the lights up too---all in all, a great weekend. Thank you for making it special. Love, A

So this is the note I should have written yesterday. You certainly take to heart the vow of "through sickness and health". I felt so taken care of by you. It's a dichotomy of feelings; on the one hand (being male and all), I don't like being fussed over, and on the other hand, I really do appreciate that you care so much for me. Your calls through the day to check how I was doing also touched me. It is why it is so easy to love you. A

One of my favourite things to do with you is the simple hug. I feel like I never want to let go. When I run my hand up and down your back and pull you tighter, it reminds me that you and I are really one in two different bodies. It is actually fun knowing that we are one experiencing separate realities. Love, Arno

Being sick is not much fun. I guess because it happens so rarely, it bothers me a bit more at times. I actually get depressed when I'm not feeling well. Your love and hugs however, really get me through much of it. You may not be the total cure for the common cold but you sure can make someone forget about its unpleasantness. I thank you for who you are and for coming into my life all those years ago. Love, PC

When we see days and days of cloudy weather, it is nice to know that I always have some sunshine in my life. When I was younger and first heard the song, probably in grade three or four, I never understood the line in the song, "You are my sunshine, my only sunshine" but since getting to know you, I get it. You really are the sunshine of my life; the bright spot of my life. I love you more than all the leaves on all the trees (well at least in the summer. I forgot, it's winter and there are no leaves on the trees.) A

Thank you for being such a wonderful support to me. I truly get how much you love me. I see it in your gentle touch, the way you hug up to me and your tender (and sometimes passionate) kisses. It is a privilege to know you, and more so, to live with you. Love, A

When I think of all the work you do to prepare for Christmas, I am really moved. You make a house look like a real home. I enjoy having family home for Christmas and look forward to cooking for them. It is you however, that is the foundation of this family. We all enjoy each other, and you are the glue that keeps everything together. No wonder I love you so much. XOXOXOXXOO; A

You really are the love of my life. Whenever I look at you, I could just hug you so much. Some women worry about how they look coming out of bed. When you get up you are just as beautiful as after you are dressed up. Well okay, the hair is a bit mad, but it adds to your loveliness. It makes you human and real. You are what I wished for as a wife long before I met you. Love, your PC

I love the way you decorate for Christmas. It is not only your vision and creativity of putting the decorations together but the love with which you do those things. Of course, it also translates into our relationship. It is filled with love and you are a big part of it. XOXOXO. Love, your PC

Well, one more sleep before Christmas. Only ½ day at work and for once, just the two of us for Christmas Eve. Perhaps a nice Christmas Movie with some egg nog and Bailey's. A little cuddle and then we get ready for tomorrow. You will be off to church tonight and I will have that cold body next to mine when you return. You will use me as your personal hot water bottle. It's all good. Love A.

I always enjoy spending time with you. Watching a bit of television and holding hands is always nice. What's nice is being beside you and being close. I enjoy reading but that does not stop us from finding time together. I also love our breakfast chats before we get into our regular routines of the day. I love you so much that the numbers of stars in the sky aren't enough. XOXOXO A

When we get busy, it seems we never have much time for each other; sort of like two ships passing in the night. When I write you these little notes it is kind of like meditation. There is nothing to think about other than you. It is you that provides the daily inspiration for writing these little notes. You are the beacon in my life that leads me to your shores. Love, A

I never get tired of telling you how much I love you. You are among other things, my best friend, a better mother to our kids than many and an inspiration to all of the family, including your siblings and cousins. Everyone wants to see what you are doing before committing themselves. I am lucky because we are on the same page mostly and I also got to marry you. Love, A

You have so many facets to your life. You are a mother, wife, grandmother, cousin, niece and a friend to dozens and dozens. They say we are blessed if we can count true friends on one hand. You do not have enough appendages to count all of your friends on. Some have acquaintances, you have friends. Before deciding what to do, they will seek you out to find out if you are going to an event, pray for them or just ask for advice. You really are blessed as am I for being privileged enough to live with you. Love, A

Over the years we have gone through many trials and tribulations that would have destroyed marriages. In hindsight, many of these issues were trivial. We tend to make big deals out of things that are not. Sometimes we can only see this with the passage of time. What was a passionate debate five years ago is simply another point of view today. Instead of being grateful for each other, we spent an inordinate time being mired in differences. Thank goodness that, over time, there is some wisdom that creeps in. I am not that strong on the institution of marriage, but I do believe the importance of staying together and working things through, no matter how emotionally upsetting it can be. There are times when things really do not work out; where lovers were just two ships passing in the night going in different directions. Those rarely wind up with acrimony though. It is usually the ones where there is a power struggle. Relationships are partnerships. Partners are equal, so there is no power grab. In the end, our commitment to each other kept us going more than anything. I have always been grateful for our family, and you as the matriarch made it all happen. It is why I love you so much. Love, A

I always like it when we go to a concert and you like it as much as me or vice versa. Having the same taste in things makes our time together special. We are different as much as we are similar. It is those differences that makes both of us grow. I learn things from you every day. Where there are differences I cannot take on, I have learned acceptance over the years. I will not, nor would I, want to change you, because then you are no longer you. Instead, I accept you unconditionally as I first found you. I just love you so much, A.

Well Christmas season is over and what a wonderful couple of weeks it was. Of course there was Christmas with dinner at your brother's house followed the next day with dinner at our house. Then there was the best present of all, the announcement that we are going to be grandparents again. We visited our good friends' house, followed by New Year's celebrations also with family and friends. Of course we then had to have our traditional New Year's Day dinner at your cousin's house followed again at friends' the next day. At least we still had a day to recover, but now it is back to work. Love, (your night in somewhat shining armour).

You are #1 in my life and have been since I first met you. Without you, I would not have had the success I have. There is a saying that behind every successful man is a woman. I don't know how true the saying actually is, as I don't know every successful man. However in your case, the saying is definitely true. You really are the rock in our relationship. You remind me of maintaining my integrity in all matters and support me in my quest to live a spiritual life. I love you — Arno

This is one of those days I wish we could just stay in bed or cozy up by the Christmas tree. It is one of those days where it is so cold, I'm just fine without having to go outside. It is one reason for becoming a consultant. However when the client expects you in, you still have to get there regardless of what the weather is. Weather like this is great snuggling weather, and there is no one I would rather do it with than you. Having you sit beside me last night reminded me how much I miss that. Love, A

I guess you didn't think I have time to write a note. Fooled you! I know sometimes I do miss a day but I try to get you a note each day. When I shovel snow I think of doing it for you. That makes shovelling so much easier. I love you a whole bunch. You are my FP. Love A

Sometimes there are things I forget to do and you step in and get them done. I too do things that at the start of our marriage was considered "women's work. You and I work in partnership and have so over the years. It is one of those things that make our marriage work so well. We have no expectations. We just do what is needed. I love you so much. PC.

All in all, it was a great weekend. Friday night with you, Saturday with friends at the Celtic concert and Sunday morning with you, some work in the afternoon and finishing with some much needed bookkeeping; then, Sunday night to the banjo special at the Hughes room with my friend Eugene. We scored a front table no less. Coming home to a nice warm bed capped off a good weekend. Best of all, you made it special. Thanks for being my wife and best friend. Love, A

This has been a lovely weekend. I had an opportunity to spend the weekend with you, friends and family. Sometimes I appreciate not having to entertain but to be entertained. So it was nice to see good friends, good food, and of course, as always, you, the icing on the cake. You will always be the main attraction to your friends and most of all, to me. Love A

I love watching you as I wake you from your deep slumber. Your expression as you awake reminds me of when waking our children when they were younger. Then you are awake and you slowly struggle to orient yourself and get out of bed, even though the radio had been on for a half hour already. That is when I love to hold you tight. You still have the warmth of sleep covering you and me, having come in from the cold, appreciate hugging up to a warm body. It makes me want to hop back in bed with you. Then reality breaks in and I help make the bed before starting breakfast. God, I love you. A

I love hugging you each morning. It is a reminder that we are connected as one. Besides, we feel good too. I once read that it is hard to argue with someone while you are hugging them. What I do know for sure is that when I hug you it expresses the deep love I have for you. You are my best friend. After all these years I still look forward to seeing you after work. Love A

What is really neat about our relationship is that each day we find ways of expressing our love for each other. Better still is that we also have independent lives. And in our case that independence does not cause us to drift apart; rather it makes us look forward to the times we spend together. Love, A

As our anniversary approaches I am reminded of our two weddings we had so many years ago. The first was to take advantage of those tax breaks that are no longer. The savings from that allowed us to buy our first new car together. Then there was the church wedding with all our friends and family. The church wedding was as church weddings usually are. It is not my thing, however, I realize how important it was not only for you but also for the parents, or as the kids fondly call us, the "rents". It was the reception that I liked most of all. We did not have one of those receptions that had three or four hundred people attend. Rather it was more like a party with close family and friends making up about sixty-five in all. We acted more like host and hostess at the time and it was beautiful with catered food and home-made food provided by our parents. The way I felt about you then has grown into an even deeper love. PC

Well, we don't seem to spend a great deal on Valentine's Day. I think the day was put in place (my thoughts are less cynical than some) to remind us of our love for each other and to find a commercial way to express that love. Because our anniversary and Valentine's Day are only separated by a couple of days, we sort of celebrate them together. Besides, I don't need a special day to show my appreciation for you. I really do that daily...little hugs, dinner and just spending time holding each other.
Love, A

Here we are, 32 years later---34 from when we first met. It seems like we have been together for such a long time, and that went by in the blink of an eye. In that blink, we managed to raise four children and watched them grow to adulthood and eventually start their own families. Being an empty nester is sort of like before having the kids; just the two of us. I am grateful that we have children and grandchildren. I am even more grateful that we never lost sight of each other. I have seen it in many relationships where the children become the main focus and the couple drift apart. Sometimes the gap becomes too wide to bridge. Fortunately we never drifted too far that it wasn't reparable. Having each other at this stage of our lives with such richness in the relationship is priceless. Love, A.

Well, another week in the books. I just read an article asking people if they would remarry their partners. A lot talked about losing that spark. Back in the seventies Werner Erhart talked about looking at things newly. The mind fights that, and looks for similarities, thus dismissing your attention to the object or thought with the notion that everything is the same except not always. That is why it is so important to come at things as though it is the first time. So instead of the relationship being thirty-two or thirty-four years old, it is as though I see you newly for the first time each morning. I love that, and I think that is what keeps our relationship fresh. Asked if I would marry my partner again, without hesitation the answer would be, "Yes"!

I'm always sad when the weekend comes to an end. Well really not sad but just that during the week we get to spend less time together. This weekend was a family weekend. It was well spent with family. The children did a really nice job with the food. It was great fun playing board games. Just sitting and chatting was also very nice. I can credit you for all your hard work over the years in keeping our family together. Your Prince Charming loves you very much.

You are the love of my life. I love when you come up to me from behind and kiss me on the neck or back. I love when you come and just sniff me after having come out of the shower. I love hugging you from behind while you are watching the sun rise, but most of all, I just love you for being you. There are a whole lot of reasons to love you, but most of all I love you just because. A

You should not feel embarrassed about how I feel about you. I do understand modesty and that too is a good quality. We do spend a lot of time beating ourselves up. For instance, if we do nine good things and one not so good, we concentrate on the one thing that did not meet our expectations, causing us to believe that we are not as good as we are. In the meantime, the nine other things that we did really well are negated. It's like a batter in baseball who hits .900 when at the plate and says, "Yeah, but I missed the other one out of ten at bats, then devotes much of his time on the strikeout instead of focusing on all the good at bats. Nine out of ten or two out of ten, you are wonderful and I love you dearly. Your PC

While I make part of your lunch each morning, it is important to note that you do a lot of little things that also contribute in so many ways. For instance you lay out the vitamin pills each morning; you water the plants and feed the cats. Mostly you clean up after me from the morning mess I make preparing breakfast and reading the paper. You also make the main portion of your lunch. I add a little at the end with the note, the yogurt and then close up your bag before leaving for work. We truly have a wonderful partnership. I love you. Arno

It never ceases to amaze me how I continue to feel about you. Judging by some of the horror stories I hear and read about from couples that have not been married nearly as long as us, I wonder if they had a chance. It is not so much about the differences in their lives because we all have differences---we are different. It is the acceptance of those differences and it is the adding up of those differences that move two individuals into one. As they say, the whole is much more than just the sum of the parts. This is our relationship. It allows our love of each other to grow and share it with others around us. We gave up on trying to be right a long time ago. Instead we remove our defences and just allow love to be there.

The weekend is almost upon us. The Blue Jays are at Spring Training and it is the end of February. There is actually hope that the winter season is turning the corner. There is promise of a heat wave next week — it is going all the way up to -5° for the high. As winter seems to be transitioning into spring, the only thing that is steady and dependable is your personality.
I love you to bits. A

I really enjoyed our "long" weekend together. You mentioned on Friday that you loved hanging out with me. I too love just hanging out with you. I'm not sure how retirement looks or if we eventually get tired of being around each other, although I can't imagine such a thing happening. I never get tired of you and I always look forward to seeing you even if it has been over 34 years from when we first laid eyes on each other. Each day is a new date for me. I love going to the movies with you. Picking up Andrea for lunch was also nice. Every time we have an opportunity to be with any of our kids it is a special treat. I love how our family turned out, and most of all, I love you. A

It is not always pleasant to spend 4 hours in the hospital's emergency ward. At least we didn't have to spend it waiting like in some hospitals. Being able to spend time by your bedside was a bit of a blessing. Usually on a Sunday, I'm up early while you sleep. I get to read the Sunday paper with a bit of a relaxing morning before you get up. This time we were both up at 5:00 a.m. and though not the best of venues, it was a nice time spending the morning with you. The morning was stretched into early afternoon as we stopped for breakfast on the way back home. I really do enjoy these moments together. There is nothing else to interfere with each other. It becomes just you and me. While they are rare moments, since we have become empty nesters, we do get more of a chance to spend time together. Your Prince Charming

Since you didn't go to work yesterday you deserve two notes today. I was sitting here eating my breakfast while you were still sleeping. I was missing you in the same fashion as though we were just dating. I felt like coming up and starting something. The love I have for you can be overwhelming at times. I am quite aware how much I love you and the emotional feelings that go with it. It is what happens when you let go and become totally committed to the relationship. Love, A

It was nice to pick you up from work yesterday. The weather was nasty and I am glad that you left your car behind. The traffic was extremely slow and I was wondering where all the traffic comes from every time there is some sort of snowfall. You make it easy to sit in traffic. I love your company and even though a normal twenty minute ride turned into a seventy-five minute ride, your presence made the time go much faster than reality. I love being your partner. A

It is Friday. When I listen to our children, the radio and many coworkers over the years, it was everyone's favourite day of the week. I used to say to them, "so, you are looking forward to laundry, housework and shopping; paying for that privilege and this is something you are looking forward to?" They must really hate their work. On the other hand, I look forward to the weekend because I get to spend it with you. It is what I enjoy even more than work. I love you. A

A Colin James concert for me on Friday, a spiritual retreat for you on Saturday and a christening on Sunday all amounted to a wonderful weekend. What was kind of cool was that I shared the concert with you; you shared your spiritual weekend with me and we got to share the christening together. It was nice to see the siblings, cousins, nieces and nephews. There are so many things we share either independently or together. That's what relationships should be about. Thank you for sharing; love Arno

Sometimes mornings can be a bit quiet. We walk around being busy and pretty soon there is an air of tension in the room. No one has said anything; there is no argument; no reason to assume anger is there. Yet, the longer there is no talking, the air is thick and communication cries out. You always seem to sense this first. You are able to open those lines of communication. So I stop and look at what is going on with me. Yes, I actually was angry that you are not getting enough sleep and that is affecting your health which is already fragile. It seems rather stupid to be angry with you because I love you and worry about your health. Sometimes we do stupid things that are completely misguided. I do love you and wish you much happiness and good health. A

Your health is still a concern to me. I really believe part of it has to do with a lack of sleep. This can cause the immune system to get run down and can also cause a bit of depression. Mind you, when you are not feeling well, that too can be depressing. I hope you start feeling better as the day goes on, otherwise I think you should come home early instead of volunteering at the Nursing Home this evening. I love you and wish you the best of health. Love A.

Well it looks like you are feeling a bit better today. It is difficult watching you not being well. I root for your well-being — for selfish reasons, I like to see you in a state of happiness all the time. I also wish you good health as I look forward to doing things together all the time. Sometimes we are like two ships passing in the early morning as we ready ourselves for work. Somehow though, we always manage to chat for a while. You always manage to regale me with interesting stories from work, and all the various dramas that occur. When you go up to exercise, I enjoy bugging you a bit, like trying to kiss you as you are lifting weights.
I know you get annoyed at that and I try not to do it too often. A

We tend to run a bit tight some mornings. This is one of those days for me, conducting interviews all day long. So this is just a quick note to say how much I really appreciate all that you do. You are my bright sunshine on cloudy days. When I am blue you provide a splash of colour and when there are days I just don't feel like doing something, you provide the encouragement, that spark that gets me going again. I love you, P.C.

I look at you and all I see is love. There are times I just love to hold you instead of going to work. This is one of those mornings. I do look forward to work and I also look forward to spending time with you. This weekend will be one of those where we will spend little time together. This evening will be spent with friends, tomorrow we are going in different directions but at least Sunday will be a day spent with the siblings, so I look forward to a little time in the evening before getting ready for another week. I really love you. A.

*This, as a lot of weekends with you was quite enjoyable.
Donnie and Andrea bought a new car, all of your
siblings and significant others met at the Markethill
Café for brunch — one of my favourite places to eat —
and enjoyed good food and chatter. Later, seeing Peta
and Eric's house was delightful. I loved the design of the
house. Now that the weekend is over, back to work. I
know we will meet up again this evening as we do every
evening since my work no longer requires me to travel.
I love you a whole bunch.
Love, A*

*Even though I was not having breakfast this morning,
it is nice to be able to chit-chat with you, or as you
like to say, have a little "guptchup" (who knows how to
spell this). I think listening to you gives me a pretty
good idea of the players at your company, including
all the opportunities for improvement. I know work
can sometimes be frustrating; more so when you see
what needs to be done. You see the silliness of some
employees and the pettiness with which they carry on.
From someone that has never engaged in that type of
behaviour, just smile and know they are dealing with
their own issues. You can observe the shenanigans as
though you were watching one of those soaps.
Love, A*

In the past, while I have changed my routine in an endeavour to get to work earlier, I noticed as I got out of the shower that you were eating breakfast by yourself. It struck me how all alone you were. I am going to have to change my routine again so that we eat breakfast together. Perhaps I will shower first, then wake you up so that we can enjoy breakfast together. I don't like to see my best friend and lover sitting all alone when it is not necessary to do so. Love, P.C.

Well I'm running late this morning but not late enough to write you a quick note to say how much I love you. There are so many things that you do where I get to know how special I am in your life. For instance the little hugs I get when stepping out of the shower, sharing your work trials and tribulations, the way you fall into my arms in the morning and the way you bless me before going to bed. They all make me feel special. It is why I love you so much and never get tired of saying so. Love, A

I love those evenings when nothing else is going on and we can just sit together with you curled up in my arms and watching a little television. A fireplace and a glass of wine with some candles would have set off the evening perfectly. We don't have a fireplace and I had a glass of wine earlier with supper, so that just goes to show you that we just need each other to set off a nice evening. What really makes it special is you.
From your PC.

Here we are, the start of another week and by the looks of it, another beautiful sunrise; another beautiful day in the making. Even though we had a hard time getting to the play at the U of T, missing the first half in the process, it did turn out to be a very nice evening. Sylvan and Mona, Sharon and your two brothers made for a memorable evening, With Andrea and Donnie coming for breakfast Sunday morning, it turned into a wonderful weekend

For someone who used to be critical of Facebook, users, you have taken to it like a cub to the jungle. Ever since I bought the iPad and the kids set you up with Facebook, it didn't take you long to contact friends from all over the world. I think it is a good thing, because I see how much enjoyment you get out of it. You also get to be in touch with people you haven't seen since your school days. I suppose it is kind of interesting to see how some of your schoolmates turned out and the wives or husbands that they married. You can share pictures with them, both old and new and it really is a nice way to catch up. You truly are an inspiration. That is why I love you so much.

There are times I marvel at your level of impatience you can exhibit at times and yet in a flash, it is over with. For instance, if I am in a slow lane while driving, you point out how you would take the faster lane. You will tell me what street to turn down and where to turn as though I had never driven a car alone before. On the other hand, you have such great empathy and compassion for people that the impatience is almost coming from another place. Without impatience, there is no patience, so we must have both in our lives, and I do understand it from time to time. So, you see, you are absolutely perfect and that is why I love you so much. Love, A

The weekend has come and gone, and a new week is upon us. I love Mondays (perhaps the only person who does). Monday is the start of the week and we get to create it however we like. Maybe it was that hit on the head from a baseball when I was ten, but I really enthuse about Monday. I wish you an equally rhapsodic day. May the troubles and controversies at work disappear like so many clouds in the sky so that all can see your sunny disposition.

Unfortunately with Kellie and her medical issues you are not getting much sleep these days. Easter is just around the corner and there is a lot to do to prepare for the twenty people we have invited for dinner. That event alone can be stressful but the lack of sleep will compound the problem. Please be sure to take care of your health as well because we all love you and don't wish for you to fall ill too. Love, A.

Well, it has been quite an ordeal for you in the past few days. Finally Kellie was able to get into surgery, even though it was at 10:00 pm last night. I know the poor girl was in so much pain prior to that. As bad as I feel for Kellie, I feel bad for you with those sleepless nights. Fortunately it is all over now and we can concentrate on Easter and the enjoyment and celebration with the family. Have a nice day. I love you — Arno

Some people are afraid of becoming empty nesters.
I always looked forward to it because I was going to
spend more time with you. I loved having the children
at home and the energy they brought transformed the
house into a loving home. Suddenly we were down
to one. My father passed away, Lisa went to B.C.,
Kellie moved into an apartment, then Natasha went to
university leaving only Andrea at home. As the kids
slowly left it had me thinking how life would be with
just the two of us, loving each other and enjoying each
other. Love, A's

Mother's Day is the one day that kids of all ages get to
honour their mothers. Yesterday was such a day for
you. By all accounts the kids did a wonderful job with
you. I think that we should celebrate Mother's Day far
more often. For the most part, I think mothers are taken
for granted for most of the year. Having Mother's Day
quarterly would allow all of us to reflect and be grateful
for the important wonders of our life. Love, A.

PS, you are equally important to me and lucky enough to
have chosen you and you me. It was a great choice
all around.

May your day be as bright and sunny as it is outside.
I don't look forward to getting the quotes on the blinds
this evening, but I suppose no day will be a good day.
At least we have the theatre to look forward to. It will
be nice to connect with some of our friends. Have a
wonderful day. I love you. A

Well, between the theatre and the blinds, we spend quite
a bit of money. I do feel it was money well spent. If
it wasn't for you, I may not have bought the blinds. I
agree though they were necessary. The white ones will
look really good in the dining room and living room
while the natural wood will be a perfect match to the
kitchen cupboards and wooden floor. You really have
good taste. Another reason to love you.

Even though I am running late today I cannot leave without a note two days running. This is just a little note to say how much I appreciate and love you. We've been together for over thirty-four years and I still can't get enough of you. I look forward to spending time with you over the coming weekend. There is enough work to do but there are the evenings. A

I'm sorry I had to leave early today so I couldn't spend more time with you. Well we are going to a play tomorrow and that will be nice. Your sibs and their families and a couple of friends. There is also a Coffee Culture place across the street we can go to after. It is going to be fun. Love A

Just as the sun is pushing through the clouds, the thought crossed as to how you truly are the sunshine of my life. I have been blessed with a lot of people in my life that have been bright spots, some shining brighter than others, but, by far, you shine the brightest and longest. Your radiant smile lights up a room. Your enthusiasm energizes all around you. I am grateful for the life we share. You have elevated my sense of love and compassion. Thank you for being you. Love, A

Well, a couple of firsts today; this is the first sheet from a brand new roll. The water I left for you is the first from a new case; and you are my first and only real love. Given the way our lives are, it is easy to drift apart. Somehow we always have time to sit and hold hands for a bit or give each other a hug and a kiss in the mornings and afternoons I look forward to warmer evenings when we can take long walks together. Later next month we can enjoy a spa weekend together with a little hike through the woods. I do love you so much. A

It was nice spending a little time with you this morning. I should make an appointment with our financial advisor to start moving some of those RRSPs. I wouldn't worry about losing your job though because God has a way of looking after us. Besides, until it happens it isn't real. It may never happen. If it does we will deal with it. The good news in all of this is that we have each other.

I am in a bit of a hurry this morning because I have to give a speech at the Annual General Meeting (AGM) today and the person preparing the speech did not have it ready on time to review. Therefore I will only have time to skim through it before presenting. I just quickly wanted to tell you I love you. Prince Charming

There are so many things to be grateful for because you do so many things and influence so many lives. Most of all I am grateful for being able to hang around you for so many years. I love your company and I love holding you. Enjoy lunch and I will enjoy you over the weekend. Love A

There are times I run behind. Unless I run really late, I will always find a way to say "I love you". I hope you enjoy your lunch and that things run smoothly at work for you. I look forward to spending a nice long weekend with you; four days away from the house with just you and I and a spa included will just be the best. It is a wonderful gift from the kids. Love, A

No matter what our disagreements may be, we always find a way to get through them. Many arguments seem to start when under duress. Whether you or I stress seems tied to the anger somehow. The good news is that we can get passed that and understand that the stress was generated under circumstances that have nothing to do with you or I; we can quickly separate issues and realize we are directing anger to the wrong place. I really don't like it when others put you in conditions of stress, whether it is the kids through thoughtlessness or some of the people you work with that appear to be self-absorbed. Love, A

Well I am off today and you are not. Being off work however is also no picnic. In many ways I envy you. I have to run around and get a new pump for the laundry room, order a cake for the shower, cut and edge the grass, gas up the car and get it washed. Then, I have to get soap for the power washer and a new hose for the shower head; then wash the deck. All this has to happen instead of developing an on-boarding package for the client, or better still, golfing. I hope you have a stress-free day so we can enjoy the theatre together. Love A.

Thank you for a wonderful weekend. It was nice to hang out with you for four full days and just be, with nothing else going on. The ride up in the cable car to the top of the mountain was grand. The five hours at the spa were the most peaceful in a long time. Even exploring the little towns by car was great. Your presence made the weekend special. Love, A

I hope you have a pleasant day and actually get to read your book during lunch. I hope you can get in to see the doctor this evening and if you do that you get a clean bill of health. After all, I want you around for a good long time. There are still a number of places we wish to go and so many things to do once we get to those places. So, enjoy a worry-free, stress-free day and I will see you when you get home. Love, A

Roses are red, violets are blue, and this is to say I love you. Well my poetic prowess is nowhere near what yours is, but I do love you and I look forward to spending some really romantic time together. I can never get or give enough hugs to you to really express how much I love you. P.C.

I don't know what made me think of it, but we really don't stay angry with each other, even when I get mad and hold on to things. You don't allow me to do that. You will ask all the questions or create a space in which I can vent---well sort of. I always take responsibility for my feelings. I don't say, "You made me angry". Mostly I say, "I am angry" when I get that way. I think that is why we have so few disagreements. All that to say, I'm glad we managed to work things out over the years, because I don't know where I would be today without you. I love you a whole bunch.

I look forward to getting away for a weekend. The reason I do is so we can hang out with nothing to do but enjoy ourselves. We can go hiking, hang out in a steam room or just spend the day in the hotel admiring each other. When we were first going out it was one of my dreams. Funny how some dreams just never change. I love you more than all the stars in the sky. A

We had a good weekend. Evita at the sold out Rose Theatre was a joy to watch. Then we got together at the Coffee Culture and that also was really nice. Family and friends gathered there for after theatre discussions and critiques. Yesterday I really enjoyed the movie, The Second Best Marigold Hotel. While watching, I tried to think which was funnier, the first or second. After supper at home we settled in to watch Andrea and Donnie's wedding video. All-in-all it was a wonderful weekend. What made the whole weekend really special was having you with me.

When I am in a hurry there is a writer's block. When thinking of something clever to say or something that might be amusing, not much seems to come forward. However, the one constant that I can always rely on, no matter the urgency or stress that happens within me, there is always you. A hug and a kiss melts all that away. I love you deeply. A

Well I did get quite a bit done this morning. It is always nice to have some accomplishments before leaving the house. For me it is a rarity but for you it is a common occurrence. I hope you enjoy your lunch, and when you have that smile on your face while eating, you give a passing thought to me, knowing I love you very much. Prince Charming.

You are the person that makes my world turn upside down at times. That first kiss had me walking around in a daze for days. I have learned to deal with that a bit better over the years (otherwise I would be broke). That's not to say that a kiss from you won't still send me over the moon. It's just the return trip is a bit faster. Love A

You are truly my sweetheart. Last night on the dance floor I was taken back to our dating days and how special it was/is just to be with you. What set me back a bit was when someone mentioned how "dapper" we looked. You looked stunning in your outfit and I wore a twenty-six year old suit. I saw neither you nor me as "dapper". The important quality is love and compassion. "Dapper" depends on someone else's taste.

While Easter has no religious significance for me, I do enjoy having family with twenty over for dinner. I must say, twenty does stretch our dining room to the limits. Andrea's wedding video was an added bonus where we can sit and reminisce. The only downside to having so much family over is the amount of clean up afterwards. But, in the end it is all worth it. From that perspective I do enjoy Easter and Christmas. They are an excuse to celebrate life with those we are closest to. I really love you and thank you for providing such a wonderful meal for so many.

The lead-up to the baby shower has been stressful. We are in the homestretch. The food has been ordered, presents bought and the only thing left is a little clean-up. The stress level should come down. I am not sure how we got into hosting a shower in the first place. I don't remember our parents putting on a shower for us — it was usually friends that put one on. But, this is what you have always done. You see a need and you take charge. We should all be grateful to you. Love, A

Well, pretty soon we will be able to put the shower behind us and then we can get on with our lives before the baby comes and then there will be other challenges. The good thing about all this is that we get to do it together. I love working with you on various projects. It is a wonderful partnership we have. I love you so much and am really grateful to be part of your life. Love, A

I look outside and I see the pool, the grass freshly cut, the abundance of birds, the green trees and I know that we are in the early stages of summer. Officially summer is not here for another month but at least we have shaken off the vestiges of winter. I look forward to these summer evenings with the nightly walks, holding hands and making comments about the neighbours' houses, gardens and simply enjoying the small things in life as we pass along the street. Love, A

It has been a busy few days. There was the baby shower
and the surprise delivery of our Grandson. Here we
were, making plans for July, and Mason decided to
arrive six weeks early. We didn't even have a chance to
fully clean up after the shower. Slowly things are getting
back to normal. You had a good night's sleep finally and
hopefully a couple more good sleeps will get things back
to normal. I love you so much, "Oma" your PC

Whether a fleeting moment in the morning or a few
minutes in the evening, it is always nice to connect.
Maybe that is part of the reason for the longevity of our
union. Of course not focusing on those things we think
the other should do differently, but focusing on our
love for each other and celebrating our differences has
always kept us connected.

I am sure you must have been thrilled to hold the new
baby and be involved in feeding the boy I noticed it was
hard for you to let go as we did not get out until a couple
of hours past visiting hours. I hope you won't be too
tired this morning as over the past week or so, sleep has
been at a premium. I suspect things will slow down for
a while and you can take a breath. Love, A

Yesterday was a short note because I was running late for a normal day, and I was supposed to be in early. This morning when I got up my eyes seemed to be more tired than the rest of me. When I got to the alarm on the other side of the room, I thought, "Okay, maybe another ten minutes", so I came back to bed. When you came up to me and hugged me, I could have stayed for ever. But then my kidneys called and when I got up again I was up to stay. All that to say that I really appreciate the little things about you — a hug here — a kiss there and always your blessings. Love, A.

It was a wonderful weekend with the beautiful orchestra and operatic singing on Saturday. Father's day yesterday was special as the kids did a really terrific job of taking care of me. An all you can eat sushi bar for lunch followed by mini golf on real grass. Then, visiting with our grandson to top of a very special day. Best of all was spending the last couple of hours with you before going to bed. Love A.

I love you beyond words or to use the expression, I love you more than my tongue can tell. I'm sorry I could not help this weekend but the government wants its pound of flesh from us. It took most of the weekend to prepare them. Love, A.

So many years have passed through that body and you still are as hot as ever. You have suffered through many things during our time together, and every time you have come to a positive outcome, including now three years cancer free. So, now it is time to enjoy this special day. You are the apple of my eye, so I wish you many, many more healthy and prosperous years. Love, A.

When I look at you, all I see is beauty. You have maintained your beauty, not because of drugs or surgery but because of the inner beauty that emanates from within you. You are loving — as witnessed by your friends, you are willing to forgive people's (including mine) transgressions and always thinking of others before yourself. We have come a long ways from our childhoods. I am so happy to be your partner in life. Love, A.

You are very dedicated and disciplined to your routines. It is a very admirable thing. Your exercises in the morning, your prayer routine, feeding the stray cats, watering the plants, cleaning up after me, followed by your morning shower. And of course, there are the kisses before we depart for work. All involving you. I am getting exhausted just thinking about all you do before you head out the door for work, Your PC.

I almost forgot to write you a note today. Having a holiday in the middle of the week is not the best because you can't always go away for a nice long weekend. You are going back and I am off tomorrow. Oh well, there is a lot of yard work which I am not looking forward to. Have a lovely day. Love, A.

I love hugging up to you and kissing you in the back of the neck. It isn't always about the sex. I enjoy holding you, kissing you and holding hands. When we went for a walk last night, I think it was the first time we did it holding hands. It is not always about power walking either. Sometimes a slower more sensual lifestyle works well too. Love, PC.

It is a bit strange and odd how little time we spend together, considering how much in love we are. A few minutes in the morning, a few minutes in the evening and sometimes only one or the other. It is why I look forward to vacations and weekends together. All that said, I am grateful to have you in my life and for the moments we spend together — they are priceless. Love, A.

A nice weekend was had by all. Kellie's fortieth birthday really was a surprise to Kellie. To have so many people show up for her birthday was a testament to your organizational skills. The visit to your brother's new place was nice and it became a really enjoyable afternoon with the siblings and their wives. I consider myself lucky to be involved with such a beautiful woman. You engage me in all the things that are important to you, and by extension have become important to me. Love, A.

You light up my life like no other. Every day I am so grateful that you have chosen me as your life partner. Some people wonder why their partners receive so many accolades or attention from others, because they see flaws. I only see the good and agree with all those that think so highly of you. I really know you better, so I can love you more. A.

Didn't get to spend much time together this morning; just the one hug. But then again, one hug is as good as a dozen or more sentences. May your day be filled with joy and happiness. May the people at your work be grateful for your presence and act just like you would like them to. Love, A.

It looks like another busy weekend coming up. The last theatre presentation until next winter and Sunday will be Father's Day. It should be fun. You are always the centre to everything that happens. Without you the theatre experience would never be as good. Without you there would be no Father's Day and without you I would not be nearly as happy. Love, A.

We got a lot done this weekend. I think you and I make a wonderful team. We got to the Master Works concert in Oakville and ran into Sylvan and Mona which is also a treat Going over to your brother's place for coffee following the concert helped capped off the evening as well. We got the deck power-washed and the outdoor furniture also uncovered and cleaned up. You got the garden going and your brother helped with trimming and pruning the trees. I did the grass cutting and dinner. All in all, a wonderful team effort. I love you so much.

This is a change. I get to leave after you today. I do enjoy getting you out of bed in the morning while you are still sleepy and stretching like the cats in the sun outside. Sometimes you almost purr (or is that a growl) when you get up. You see, it doesn't always have to be the big things. I do appreciate the little things too. Love, A

I was reading how the government appointed a couple of judges to the Ontario Court of Appeals. Obviously there are some politicians and religious leaders that are hung up on legal definitions. I didn't get married to you based on some definition of whether it should be between a man and a woman. We got married because we loved each other and marriage was a way of recognizing that commitment. To restrict allowing people to express that love is, in my mind very antiquated. It was man that made the rules and then used the bible to justify their homophobia. Personally, I love you regardless of how our institution defines us. Love, A

Sometimes I think that if I let you, you would sleep well into the morning — much like Sundays. On Sunday though, I do not set the alarm for you. During the week it is always set for the same time yet most days you manage to sleep through it. I actually don't mind waking you because I get to stand there at times and just observe how beautifully you sleep and how peaceful you appear. It seems a shame to wake you but then again, obligations are what gets us going when it is the last thing we want to do. Once we get going though, we are usually grateful that we are up and accomplishing things instead of wasting the day away. I do love you a whole bunch and enjoy those special moments. Love, A.

You are my sunshine (I guess there is a song about that).
On such a cloudy, warm muggy rainy day, you are still
the brightest thing in my life. I love you dearly and can't
wait to spend more time with you. Have a great day and
enjoy your lunch. Love, A.

What a nice weekend. Even though quite busy on
Saturday and Sunday morning preparing for our
annual family picnic and in spite of the forecasted
thunderstorms, it really went well. Yesterday was a day
of just kicking back and relaxing. This is why we do it on
a long weekend. A short week and then off to a wedding
next week. Enjoy the week at work. Love, A

Two more sleeps and we are off for a nice relaxing
weekend. I am looking forward to a little "us" time. In
the meantime, I wish you a wonderful day and hope you
prepared yourself a delicious meal that you are enjoying
while reading this note. I love you more than all the stars
in the sky and more than my tongue can tell. Love, A

A little love note to say, what else, I love you!! I really enjoy holding you. Your body seems to melt in my arms. Flowers are nice but they just don't seem to last as long as I love you. At best, they can only be a temporary expression of how much I love you. Love in the real sense is a day-to-day commitment. I am committed to you in the same way. Love, A

When we look out of the kitchen, we see our huge willow tree, the grass and the smaller plants struggling to become trees. Since our kitchen faces the front, we also see the expanse of grass to the road and more trees across the street. It is a peaceful scene, and when I see you with a bowl of porridge looking out at the birds, it does make for a serene morning. May your day be as peaceful as your morning. Love, A

The concert with Fraser and Girard was really quite something. The CD launch and the intimate atmosphere of the Hugh's Room made it really special. I am sure you had an equally special time spending is with Donnie and little Mason. I am glad that the Indian food was a success and enjoyed by all. Have a nice day, love A.

It has been a busy week for both of us, both at work and away from it. I look forward to spending some time with you over the coming days. I hope you have a peaceful day at work and an enjoyable evening out with your "peeps". I love you madly and wish we had the day off to go on a road trip and picnic. Love, A.

I just heard a line in a song that made me think of you "When I see your face I think you're amazing." It is how I feel about you too. You are the icing on the cake of life. I love you so much and with the many things you do; you touch so many lives in so many ways. You have so many that want you, I feel privileged to be with you. Love, A.

It is nice to get out once in a while during the week. I am glad we had the opportunity to see Rick Mercer at the Rose Theatre with our friends. We really enjoyed the show and a lovely chat with our friends at Coffee Culture following the show. I enjoy watching you interact with friends. No matter where we are, you somehow wind up the centre of attention. Not because you seek it but others, me included are fascinated with you. Love, A.

It was a beautiful day. It is too bad that you are
working. It would have been a nice day for a road trip
or to just go somewhere for an extended weekend. Be
that as it may, I'm glad we had some time to chat last
night and this morning. I always love holding you,
especially while you are still in your PJs. Love, A.

One can only hope all works out well at work and that
they are able to pay you. I know it can get somewhat
stressful for you — not knowing if you will get paid. And
then there is the office politics that no one should be
required to put up with. I find it incredible that people
want to complain to you because the owner doesn't have
the courage to deal with his employees directly. Well,
there are those wonderful times we spend together, and
that can make up for some of the nonsense you have to
put up with. Love, A.

I enjoyed spending a quiet Sunday with you. I couldn't help but think of you when I was typing some of the notes I send you. Because I type them into the computer, sometimes weeks later, I am reminded how I feel about you and it makes me rethink of how grateful I am to have you in my life. I think by writing these notes I don't take you for granted because I am always thinking about all the wonderful things you do and the fantastic person you are.

In the morning you stand in front of the kitchen window with your bowl of porridge and watch the birds eating. It is such a peaceful scene, and I sense that it is a very meditative practice for you. I enjoy coming behind you during times like that to give you a hug and just hold you. It is just so nice to be in love with such a wonderful princess. Love, A.

I do enjoy shopping with you (Other than when it's aimless window shopping). It reminds me of our connection and the choices we make together. It is a beautiful partnership. I love you and am constantly grateful for being a part of your life. I wish you a wonderful day and enjoy lunch. Love, A.

Another beautiful day today. I want to have this day be all about you as we prepare for our annual picnic. While I don't look forward to the preparation and cleanup, it is always satisfying to see thirty to forty people thoroughly enjoying themselves. Too bad that only one of the kids will be there. Nonetheless, it will be a great event because you are there. Love, PC

Norma, I am hoping that all is fine with you. On the other hand, I do wish they can find out why you are getting these constant headaches. When we got married, we made a pact to grow old together. Well, we are far from being old. I guess it is all relative since our kids believe we are old already. I am sure the grandchildren think we are even older than that. Have a wonderful day and know that I love you no matter what. Love, A

Entertainment city this evening; I will do my best to help you get ready for it. In the meantime, I hope you have a wonderful day at work. I really love you and wish we could spend more alone time, but those are the trade-offs for having a wonderful and large family. Love, A

I cannot express enough how much I appreciate you every day. Now that the warmer weather is here, I appreciate sitting outside with you and enjoying a meal on the deck. We do our own thing during most of the week and yet we are never apart emotionally. Going to a play on Saturday, followed by an outdoor movie with popcorn and hot chocolate is always a treat. Having those movies right downtown in the square is pretty neat.

While watching Jose Feliciano last night and holding hands with you put me into quite a state of bliss. Jose's music was wonderful and what a gentleman. Talking to him after the show was special. Watching him sitting there in the lobby while he allowed people to come up to him and take pictures, showed me just what a special fellow he is. Having you there and enjoying the evening put me over the top.

I know I have missed a couple of notes due to leaving early. I want you to know, it does not diminish my love for you. Have a wonderful day and a peaceful lunch. I will be thinking of you while on the golf course. Love, A.

It is hard to express at times how much I love you. Just holding you close means so much to me. Because of how busy we are, we don't get to do it enough. However, I suspect if we have too much of a good thing, we take it for granted. You are a very special lady that I never want to take for granted. I love you madly. A

Just a quick note to tell you how much I love you. Sitting together in the small "meditation" room of yours was really nice. It is such a cozy little room and to spend it with you just before going to bed was kind of special. You have managed to transform a "karate" room from Natasha's days to one that just exudes love and peace. Love, A

Just a quick note to say I love you and have a great day. May Burton Manor and bible studies be a great experience as always. I know you usually give more than you get. Love, A

I love you. Enjoy the day at work. As Christmas approaches, most things are done, so we can start to relax a bit. Love, A

On this dreary morning you are the sunshine in my life. All things become much better with you in my life. I love hugging you — a ritual we have after making the bed. I love those kisses as you step out of the shower. While there are many things to do in the morning, you are always there to support me and follow up on those things I miss. We do make a wonderful team. Love, A

As fall's grip loosens to give way to winter, it is good to snuggle up to you. Your warm and smooth skin against mine is the best. The closeness to you reminds me how strong our love really is. The things I do and have done in the past remind me of the self-absorbed person I was before meeting you. Sharing a life together makes us both grow.

It was nice to be home this morning so I could make you roasted potatoes, liver and onions for lunch. It was well worth the effort. You are easy to do things for. I love you like no other. You should have a wonderful day today. While Christmas is rapidly approaching, there are still a number of things to take care of. Thinking about them can be overwhelming. We have to focus on one thing at a time, accomplish one thing each day, so that by Christmas, everything is done.

I love it when we can spend time with friends such as we did last night. While these are our friends, they were spawned through your interaction at church and the ancillary groups. They became "our" friends through you and it just goes to show the type of person you are to have such quality of friends. When I see how much your friends adore you, I am equally grateful that I have as lovely a wife as you. Love, A

As we get ready to go to the Dobell's it is somewhat a mixed blessing. On the one hand we get to spend a wonderful evening with friends; each year it is a most enjoyable experience. On the other hand, it takes away from getting Christmas preparations completed. But, as in every year past, we always seem to pull it together. Enjoy the day at work and know that I love you. A

So, the other day, I was thinking why so many relations go south once the kids are born. The focus becomes them (the children) and vying for their attention. The relationship between husband and wife starts to deteriorate into "I'm right" and "You're wrong." We spend so much time defending our positions and so much animosity is built up that we turn to our children for affection. Fortunately, for the most part, our relationship has always come first. One can only bring up healthy and happy kids if the relationship with the parents is solid. Since the kids have grown up and left, we are not strangers to ourselves. We have not become those who merely tolerate each other because we are too scared to venture out on our own or fail to fix the relationship because it is easier to ignore. Love, A

A note to say I love you. Not much to say this morning, but that does not mean that you are any less in my thoughts. Indeed, seeing you in your PJs reminds me of your warmth and cuddliness. Tonight will be interesting as we try William's sushi restaurant. The limited reviews of the place have been very good. It is also a good opportunity to catch up with those I have worked with, in a more social setting and to introduce you to some of my new colleagues that have started since last year. Love, A

Sometimes even if the food is not quite to your taste, the company at dinner was wonderful. I know you enjoyed the "cooked" fish and the desert so I made up the difference by getting stuffed with all the various raw fish, caviar and the wine pairings. In the end, I found having you beside me was the best. You can now also put faces to the names of those I work with. Love, A

Love, love, love, that is what our relationship consists of. We have love for our friends, children and each other. Maybe that is why we also enjoy life as much as we do. Living is a privilege and when we view it that way, it really makes everything richer. If only they taught kids how to live life in schools---ah well, enjoy the day. Love, A

I will try to be a bit more mindful in ensuring there is enough for you to have some choices for lunch. I hope you have a wonderful day. You have done a lot of work and running around this week. You deserve to have an easier day. May blessings be upon you and that things turn out exactly as you intended. Love A

I am really excited about you being in my life. Even though we have been together for thirty-four years, I still feel like being on a second date at times. I love the notion of hanging out with you. After all these years, I still feel the same. I always wanted a happy marriage and I got exactly that, thanks largely to you. Love, A

When I look at you, I see the beauty in you. It is something that radiates from within you and does not always come through in pictures. While you look good in them, I think you look much better in person. In person we get all of you, your physical beauty as well as your inner beauty. Sometimes pictures do not capture the inner beauty---I do. Love, A

I guess the time has come to focus on Christmas. The first week of Advent has come and gone, so it is time to get those outside lights up and to scope out where to put the tree. All these things can be very stressful. Christmas time I have noticed affect people differently. There is a trick that I have employed when getting stressed. Since the physical sensations of stress are similar to that of excitement, we can chose to be either excited or stressed. I chose the former, so when you feel stressed, tell your brain that you are not stressed but excited. So, we are in for exciting times. Love, A

We spent a nice weekend. The soirée and theatre made the weekend somewhat special. Adam and Natasha returned from Florida with Adam's parents Sunday and we got to spend some time with them before heading back to Orillia. We got to hang out Saturday evening together. Now it is time to start focusing on Christmas because heading towards it can sometimes be stressful. Love, A

I really appreciate all your support. I know you have not been feeling well lately. Having that accident left me a bit depressed; then you came along and gave me a big hug and said, "I love you" and that, "The car can be fixed" meant so much to me. Thank you for your love and understanding. As much as I feel bad for having damaged the car, your hugs and feelings made a bad situation much better. I love you too. A

Another show this evening, Kinky Boots. It has a lot of good reviews and so has the restaurant. Good food, a good show and most of all, I get to spend it with you. You are, as the expression goes, the icing on the cake, or the ketchup on the fries, or the mustard on a hot dog. Okay, enough with the similes. I love you. A

Red seems to be the colour of love and anger. So in anger, cheeks turn red or blush in infatuation; we wave red capes at angry bulls to get them angry enough to chase us. We can have blankets with red hearts that symbolize love; the apple represents both temptation (mostly in biblical terms) yet for many other countries it is a symbol of love. Valentine's Day is filled with red symbols all depicting love. Red arrows, red cards, chocolate boxes decorated in red and the ubiquitous red hearts and red roses. All this to say I couldn't find a blue pen this morning, and to express my love for you., A

It is nice to know that we will be spending a lot of time together this weekend. Two concerts back to back; I think it is the first time that has happened. May our weekend be filled with joy and happiness. Love, A

It is a week before Christmas and we are starting to move ahead with plans and decorations. I know it is a holy time for you and your siblings. For me it is a wonderful opportunity to spend time together and watch the wonder of Christmas light up the children's eyes, even though they are much older. Little Mason, the newest grandchild addition, is still a bit too young, but by next year that too will bring joy into our lives. Love, A

I am sorry I missed you last night. We usually have a bit of time to talk. I was just too tired to wait. However, it is nice to wake up beside you. You are the pearl of pearls in the seas. You stand out above all the rest. Your compassion for others uplifts all those around you. Your willingness to spend time with the lonely in a seniors' home, the way you talk to those about to enter surgery, all those thinks make you a special woman. While your friends see you once in a while, I am fortunate to see you on a daily basis. I am truly grateful to have you in my life and share our experiences with each other and the rest of those around us. Love, A

Thank you for all the support this weekend. It was much needed and appreciated. I love you from here to Pluto and back. A

Sometimes we get caught up with issues that affect not only us, but others as well. While it can be upsetting and hurtful, at the end of it all, if we can't let go, it only hurts us. The person causing the hurt may be totally oblivious to the other's feeling and then carry on as before. During times such as these, it is difficult for me to find ways of supporting you. I am always stuck in the helplessness of not knowing what to do. What I do know is that I truly love you. A

I love you so much. Sorry in a rush so I don't have time to construct a really good note. Love, A

Not too much of a note for you today — too busy, running late, but not too busy to say I love you. Have a nice lunch. Love, A.

Have a wonderful day and enjoy your evening. I will be in the gym and then do some running around trying to get ahead of the crowd for shopping now that pretty much everyone is back to work. I hope you will have an easier and less stressful day at work now that everyone should be back. I love you a whole bunch.

You always look so great, even in your PJs. In the end, I think it has very little to do with your physical looks (although that's great too) but your inner looks so to speak. I don't find much of a difference after all that makeup and hair combing or when you first role out of bed. For me it is the inner feeling that attracts me so much. Of course that is not to say that you are not physically beautiful too. It is what compels one to break the ice and talk. It is the inner beauty that sustains us. Love, A

Sometimes I feel like a giddy kid about to go on his first date. I'm not sure if there are many others that feel that way after thirty plus years of marriage. Even today, it still feels like puppy love. I hope you have a wonderful day at work and enjoy your lunch. Love, A

I love you to bits. I love when you first get out of bed, still sleepy-eyed and slightly disoriented, looking for a hug right after we finish making the bed. It seems that you need a good hug to start the day and I am happy to provide it. I must say, it is a wonderful way to start the day. Love, A.

Well, another red letter day. I don't know where those damn pens hide themselves. Thank you for a wonderful weekend. I always enjoy spending time with you. May your day be a continuation of the weekend. May it be joyful and full of happiness. May your lunch be uninterrupted and peaceful. Love, A

May you have a peaceful and productive day at work. I know you bring joy to all those round you. So, my wish is that all those that benefit from your presence return the favour and bring you joy. May work be a joyous occasion this day. Love, A

It is nice to see that you need two hugs some days. It is nice to be needy, but not too needy. You are a strong and independent woman most times but you are also sensitive and vulnerable at times. It is good to know we can depend on each other during those times. I think that's what makes our marriage such a good partnership. Have a wonderful day at work and enjoy your lunch. Love, A.

I do love those early morning hugs before going to work. It will be nice to go for dinner even though it will be a cast of thousands for Dave's 80th birthday. I really enjoy being with you, regardless of where it is. Perhaps we are due for another spa session. Maybe we should go up to Owen Sound a day ahead of the wedding and just spend some time together. Love, A

It was wonderful having all the kids over last night. I am especially grateful for Natasha making the two hour trip and then again leaving at 9:30. It must have been an exhausting day for her. You are such a trooper too, hosting all those people, especially after a long day at work already. Enjoy the evening. Love, A

It has been a nice week and weekend. I got to spend time with you, entertain your relatives and just enjoy being. You really are the centre of my life. I couldn't help looking at you from a distance while you were engaged with others. I saw the beauty within you and wondered how I would get to know you if I didn't already. I am so lucky. Love A

A week to go before leaving for Cuba. I am already excited. Not only do I get to spend exclusive time with you, but we also get to see Havana, a city stuck in the fifties and sixties. It is a tragedy what happened to Cuba all because they had the temerity to overthrow a corrupt government held up by American interests. Today, the revolutionists would be called terrorists. All because someone labels them that. Sorry, on my soapbox again. Love A.

I am excited to have you all to myself for the whole week. No work, no bible study, no Burton Manor, no night out with the girls, just you and me. We don't get away often enough, but that is what makes it special. After all, too good a thing is not as good as we might wish it to be. Have a wonderful day and a lovely lunch. Love, A

I just love hugging up to you, especially in the mornings while you are still warm, just coming out of bed. I love hugging you from behind while you stare out at the birds. In the mornings it is quite peaceful, even with the radio on. You are still at ease and peace before the busy day kicks in. Soon we will leave all this for a different enjoyment, a trip away.

Yesterday Jayne asked if I was excited to be going on vacation. I told her that I only start getting excited once I pass through airport security. I must say though, I can feel the excitement in my belly already. There are only two more sleeps left. I suspect the next couple of days will be filled with stress as we clear our calendar of work and get ready for the trip. I hope your day will be a relaxing one. Love, A

Within 24 hours of you reading this, we will be preparing to leave for Cuba. The weather is awesome — sort of like when we went to Hawaii in December. There is no point in worrying if you have a job when you return. It is a company that has been careening from one problem to another disaster to the next. The stability reminds me of that of a ball in a pinball machine, bouncing from one thing to the next. Worrying about something you have no control over is rather pointless. We have survived many other issues as well, so there is no reason to believe we will not survive this as well.

We have had a wonderful holiday. It seems they are
never long enough. There is something special when
there is nothing to worry about other than just being.
The staff was wonderful and they all made sure we
were their special guests. Driving through Cuba was a
wonderful experience. I marvel at people that have so
little and can be so happy while those that have so much
seem unhappy. Makes me wonder if we are chasing the
wrong dreams. I love you more than all the snowflakes
on the ground.

Before falling asleep last night and before you came
to bed, I was thinking about you and how you were
already beside me. It was like I could feel your energy
beside me. I miss you when you are not beside me and
I also know we need our space. I think that is why our
relationship works so well. Love, A

It was a wonderful day with you yesterday. I was a bit disappointed that you were not feeling better though — not for me, but for you because I know how much you enjoy an outing to the big city. Well, we are back in Toronto in a couple of weeks. Hopefully by then you will be much healthier and we can really enjoy the day together. I love you lots. A. There are only so many ways to love you, or so the saying goes. Well, I haven't got the "so many" as yet. Each day I find new ways to love you. Sometimes it is just a touch, other times it is your insight and still another is to watch you interact with the kids. Your PC

Sometimes the morning just gets away from you. I am determined that is not going to happen again. This is just a little note to say how much I love you. Enjoy your lunch. Hopefully you will not be disturbed today while having your lunch. Maybe a nice walk is in the cards for you. It will get you out of the office and away from the turmoil.

I really love you. I love to touch you and help with dressing you sometimes. I enjoy the challenge of figuring out what fruit I should cut up for your lunch and trying not to be repetitive to the point of boredom. I love holding you, hugging you and enjoy those kisses that send electric shocks through my system. Enjoy your day, love, A.

I love hugging you especially with your soft nightgown.
Standing by the window eating your porridge and
watching the birds in the front yard looks from here,
almost meditative. You seem so peaceful. Hugging you
from behind seeks to transfer some of that peace and
love to me. It is nice to start the day in that fashion, as
I know how hectic your day can be. I love you! Have a
great day. Love, A XOXO

Sometimes we are passing ships as you so aptly pointed
out this morning. We have to see each other from our
respective decks, longing to be with the other. At least
we know both ships will dock on the same pier. It also
means that regardless of how much or little time we get
to spend, we still love each other so much.

Our two ships finally docked last night. I enjoy the
evenings when we can hang out together. You are an
amazing partner. It was great having you and me
watching a baseball game together and holding hands.
I do love you; have a nice lunch. XOXO A.

Since I missed writing a note yesterday, I thought I better do it today. Yesterday I didn't write a note because we traveled to work together which was a real joy. As in weekends, I love taking road trips with you, regardless of the destination, short or long. It is just you and me in close proximity. Have a great day. Love, A

Wow, what a weekend! You really have a knack for pulling me out of moods. I was a bit out of sorts with all the dogs around and even though you were not crazy about them running around either, you did not let it affect you. There are two things that drive me to distraction, one is unruly kids who are left to run around by their parents, and the other are unruly dogs that are left to run around by the owner. I don't dislike dogs, it is the owners and how they react (or fail to) when their dogs get rambunctious. That my dear, drives me to distraction. Yet you manage to pull me away from the distraction to still enjoy the weekend and not make it about the dogs or their owners.

As I watch you lying on the floor in the mornings doing your exercises, thoughts go through my head of carnal pleasures that I would change the type of exercise you experience. I am unabashedly in love with you and at times it seems as though I cannot get close enough. Love, A

It was a nice evening last night. Most of all I enjoyed driving there and back with you. The food was terrific as usual and spending time with your siblings and their spouses was also a treat. Perhaps it is because we see things similarly that I enjoy our talks on the way home from most events or journeys. I love you, A

Today is a sad day, yet a happy one. It is the last day we will be going to Eric's Restaurant as he has sold it. On a happy note, we are going to Eric's restaurant to enjoy his cooking one more time. His restaurant has survived over many others but unfortunately it still did not make enough money. They managed to keep the place afloat for so many years, I can only imagine that it must have taken a load off both him and Peta. Going there will be bitter sweet, and you are the sweet part. Love, A

I am glad that you are feeling much better. It would suggest that the symptoms you had on Monday may be the result of your anticipated CT scan. Sometimes the stress does not manifest itself until the stress has past. I enjoy sitting here in the kitchen writing these little notes because it causes me to think of you and how much I really love you. To others these notes may seem corny or maudlin, but it is just me, expressing my love to you. I guess when you are truly in love it can seem a bit corny, but oh well. Love, A.

A new book to immerse yourself into. I hope you will enjoy it as did I. In fact I a finished the entire box, mostly by reading through lunch. Enjoy your lunch and your evening. As you do, remember that I love you. A

I hope you have a nice lunch today. While writing in Kellie's fortieth birthday card, I am reminded of your for fortieth that we celebrated at this house. Your aunt wanted to throw a surprise party and there were too many guests, so she had to have it at our place, under the guise of celebrating a friend's birthday. There you were, wanting to help with the set-up and it was all I could do to take you away from the house. My, my how time moves along. It seemed like only a few years ago. I guess that is because we are still young at heart. Love, A

I really enjoy cuddling up to you. Last night was special because we sat together holding hands and watching the Blacklist preview for the upcoming season and a bit of baseball before the night turned into an endless ringing of telephones. All in all though, it was a pleasant way to spend an evening. Enjoy your lunch and book. Since the Toronto International Film Festival is over, I guess the office should be getting back to normal — hopefully. I love you a bunch. A.

I love you and hope everyone in your office feels the same way. If they do, maybe they will make your day at the office a lot easier. You deserve that because you have done so much for them over the years. Enjoy the lunch you made yourself and just imagine a nice hug from me.

May you enjoy you lunch and the day. Perhaps go for a walk; after all, there won't be too many days like today left. Pretty soon you won't be able to see those garden gnomes on all those tacky lawns, lol. Hopefully you will have a day to be remembered in a good way of course. Then you can take that happiness and spread it throughout the seniors' home.

You are the most important person in my life. I always look forward to spending time with you, whether sitting next to me, holding hands and watching television or spending the weekend away, or simply heading out on a road trip. Sometimes one's best friend is also his or her spouse. I have known some that just can't wait to get out of the house to be with friends. I know there is none better than you. Enjoy your lunch. Love, A

I love you and look forward to the weekend. Love, A

Even with the number of people we had in this weekend, the house looks fantastic. I think if it wasn't for you, the house would look a little more like my office, or my apartment when we first met; that is, stuff everywhere. You are the one that makes our house look cozy and I am very grateful for that. I love you beyond all else. A

Planning a vacation with you or for you is always fun. It is a joy to watch you discover new countries. I enjoy sharing new experiences with you. It is really a joy to know we share and enjoy so many of these together. I believe it is important to get away every once in a while, whether for a couple of weeks or just a weekend. There are no other daily distractions — only to share joyous experiences. Love, A

On a gloomy day such as today, it is nice to have you in my life. You are the sunshine on a dull day. On other days you are the inspiration for leading a joyful life. I am lifted up when I am down because your perspectives give me pause to look in other directions instead of being self-absorbed. Thank you for being my life partner and bringing so much richness and sunshine into my live. Love, your PC.

It has been a long week already and is only the first day back. It feels good to see Donny recovering from surgery faster than expected. Hopefully you can recover as quickly from the stress of the past few days. We will visit Donny again today and again on the weekend. Then we will enjoy Thanksgiving. We really do have a lot of things to be thankful for, including our family and the extended family. Love, A.

You really are the bright spot in my life, regardless of weather. You brighten my days when I am gloomy and you never let my moods affect you other than to pull me up when needed or to admonish me when I am being selfish or self-centered. You are my constant reminder of what human beings aspire to. Love, A

Well, Thanksgiving is almost upon us and I will start my "thanksgiving" early. I am thankful that I met you; I am thankful that we started conversing so many years ago; I am thankful for having invited you to an est seminar, as it led to our first kiss. I am thankful you married me. I am thankful for having, raising and guiding our children so that they become the wonderful adults they are. I am thankful you stuck with me through the rough spots, and most of all I am thankful I get to hug you each day. Love, A.

Another weekend; another opportunity to spend time with you. There is also the theatre and concert season. Our first concert of the new season is tomorrow and that is always exciting. In spite of all the turmoil going on at work, don't let yourself get drawn in. Enjoy your lunch, tune out the noise and be at peace with yourself. Love, A

Every once in a while, we get so busy in the morning concentrating on what we need to do, there is no time to talk about things. Well, at least we have a routine where we make the bed together followed by a hug and kiss. Through these notes I get to tell you how much I love you too. Love, A

It is always wonderful to just hold you and hug you. It is such a warm feeling. It reminds me of our connection which is much deeper than just physical. Sometimes we imagine a God that has a physical form. While our emotions are certainly physical sensations, as are feelings, there is a much deeper sense of love at play, beyond all those wonderful sensations. I really believe that is where God really resides. God is love, not some human sitting on a cloud or chair next to his son. Off on a bit of a tangent this morning I see. Love, A.

For once there was nothing to do this weekend. No obligations, no visitors, just you and me. The only deviation was to look after your friend Daniel, who is far too young to be so sick. I do wish him a speedy recovery and hope his life gets back to normal. Enjoy the day. Love, A

I love when you cuddle up to me in the middle of the night. I like feeling your warmth when we hug first thing in the morning and the last hug in the evening. The closeness in physical terms also brings us closer in connecting on the spiritual plane as well. Love, A

What do you know; after twenty-eight days of posturing, the election is finally here. I will send you directions. In the meantime, have a wonderful lunch and enjoy your day. Also know that I love you and wish you a wonderful and peaceful day. Love, A

You are my rock, you keep me on the straight and narrow when I tend to wonder off my spiritual path. You are there to remind me when things are not working and how they can be fixed. It continues to reinforce how lucky I was to find you. Love, A.

On this foggy morning I can see clearly for miles how much I love you. You are such a warmth and comfort. You provide that whether we are in the dead of winter or in the middle of summer. I love you more now than when we first met all those years ago. Who knew that was even possible. Love, A

Back to work. Sadly all good things come to an end. Thank goodness for having the past couple of weeks fill our memory banks with so many pleasant thoughts and experiences. I hope the first day back to work is not stressful for you and there is no huge backlog.
I love you madly. A

Have a nice day. I look forward to the weekend. Saturday evening looks like a quiet evening. I have a few meetings scheduled throughout the day but should be back at a reasonable hour. Enjoy the evening and I will look forward to seeing you when you get home. Love, A

When we got married, I had no idea of how wonderful marriage could be. We had children not because we just wanted them or it was the thing to do, but because we wanted to have them to be an expression of both of us. How cool would it be to have children who share the best of our good qualities? And so it came to pass. Perhaps some inculcation of other habits also sprouted forth. To have an expression of us presented to the world is not a bad thing. The kids are out making a difference, and that is all we could ask of them. The kids have flown the coup so to speak, but we still have each other and our enduring love. A

Another good weekend behind us. Saturday, getting ready for Sunday, some cooking; then Sunday your aunt coming to see all the Wilson side of the family, and at the same time celebrating Natasha's thirtieth birthday. All in all, a great weekend, and it all started by an idea you cooked up a few weeks ago. Have a great day,
Love, A.

On cold mornings such as this one, it is especially nice to hug — body warmth. I was thinking of special moments in my life and two really stuck out — aside from meeting you and the kids being born, as they were all special moments. There was the time while still living on Sheppard Street and my mother and I were sitting on chairs on the veranda of our penthouse. It was after we had gone to visit you and Natasha in the hospital shortly after she was born. What made it special was how candid she had been about her personal life. It was really the first time she opened up to it, and I could tell that she may have regretted some of her life, as she appeared quite sad. As you know, my mother was always such an upbeat person, something that I picked up from her. She would not let the circumstance in her life dictate how she felt. However, there seems to come a time when reflecting, it was not how she imagined her life to turn out. Then she was fine and we went on to other topics. That conversation stuck with me because it made it okay to have regrets. It also taught me that we should not wallow in them, but acknowledge them and move on. But I digress. The other was the time I was introduced to your mother. You had been to my humble abode in downtown Toronto, and we wandered over to Kensington Market as you had not seem it before. We ended picking up crabs for $0.25 each and yet you were convinced that you could have got them for $0.20 each. Ah well, we then took the car to your place because you wanted to introduce me to your mother. She was warm and I could tell right away that she had a heart of gold. No wonder her daughter came from that line. Then she took those crabs from you and made the most amazing and delicious curry that I had experienced thus far. The apartment that your mother lived in was so filled with love and family. I knew I was in the right place. Love, A

I have a conference call this morning and then will head out to book our weekend and pick up some fruit for your mid-morning snack. I am looking forward to attending "A Night to Remember" with Presley, Perkins, Lewis and Cash. Not that they will be back from the grave any time soon mind you, but it should be fun. Have a lovely day. Love, A

It is such a joy to get up early in the morning and prepare one of you favourite meals for lunch. For me, it is a way of saying, "I love you". While some people hate cooking, I find it to be another way of expressing love. That is what motivates me to cook for family and friends. Enjoy your lunch and know it was made with much love. A

I guess you do read these notes, given you looked all over for yesterday's non-existent note to no avail. Oh well, here is one. We work within a five minute drive yet miles apart in what we do. It seems I got lucky with the people I work with. Enjoy your lunch and the rest of the day. Love, A

Another weekend is upon us. All the various Christmases are now finished. Catholic, Protestant, Coptic and Eastern Orthodox, all done. It was time to take the decorations down and place them into the various boxes and back into the basement storage area. There is so much anticipation that begins to build shortly after Thanksgiving and runs right up to Christmas Eve. Then, in almost a blink of an eye, it is over. Keeping the decorations up through the various Christian Christmases allows the season to be stretched a little further. I hope you have a nice day.

Yesterday you missed out on getting one of my notes, and I missed telling you how much I love you. I'm glad we had so much alone time last night. It is always nice to spend an evening together, even if it was watching Agent Carter kick some butt. We actually will have quite a busy year coming up. There is the weekend at the Mohawk Inn, then there is the weekend in Algonquin Park, followed by a Seattle to Alaska cruise, perhaps a trip into the Tuscany to watch our nephew get married and then Natasha's wedding somewhere north of Orillia. That only takes us to September. I may be working a lot longer that I thought. LOL. Love, A

This has been a really nice weekend. Dancing in the living room, just hanging out on Saturday and spending time with daughter, son-in-law and grandson. We even face-timed with one of the other children. All in all a lovely weekend culminating with some quiet time off. Enjoy the day. Love, A

You are my sunshine, my only sunshine. That's because you are such a bright person — both mentally and physically. Mentally because you are so smart both emotionally and intellectually. On the physical side, well you are good looking, you wear nice clothes and you carry yourself well too. The bright colours you wear certainly remind me of bright sunshine. You just brighten up the place on a dull and dreary day such as this one. Love, A

I love you more than all the raindrops outside. Your gentle kisses, that amazing body and most of all that wonderful mind of yours that never stops loving people. Your compassion and love are reflected in everything you do. I also love the way you do not suffer fools. You do it in such a way that dismisses them so that they get the message and walk away feeling better about themselves. Love, A

I always felt odd using or hearing the word sweetheart. Mostly, when growing up I heard it used more in a derogatory way, as in, "Yeah — he's a real sweetheart", meaning the opposite. The more we are together, the more the meaning has changed for me. You really are a sweet-heart and the love that pours out from you brings a warm glow all over you. Love, A

I can't express enough how much I love you, and love you I do. There are of course the big things such as the new Blackberry you got me, (the one you fondly call the "Blueberry"). Then there was the clothing trip to Harry Rosen's to upgrade a ten year old wardrobe. But I love the little things too, such as watching you watch the birds, that extra squeeze you give me when holding hands, the extra food you make so that others have some to take home, and on and on it goes. You are a lovely human being. I am glad I get to share all this and so much more. Love, A

It is really nice to spend each and every morning with you before we head our separate ways. I always look forward to evenings as well, when we reconnect before finally heading to bed. I am looking forward to visiting Kellie's new place and catching up with her in-laws. They are wonderful people and I enjoy spending time with them, as do you. Love, A.

Thank you again for a lovely weekend. When I think about it, any weekend with you in it is a wonderful weekend. You are just so cool to hang out with. It was also nice to see Kellie and Zar's new house, and well worth the wait. Having her in-laws just added to a wonderful evening. Love, A

Sometimes there just isn't much to write about; nothing to amuse you while having lunch. So I am glad you always have your book to fall back on. May your lunch be more than just filling your tummy. When eating fish, I thank it for giving up its life to provide me with the energy needed to sustain my body. I do this with plants as well and to all those that have had a hand in making the food I eat. That way it becomes a powerful connection to all. Well, for someone who didn't have much to say, I did manage to ramble on. Enjoy your lunch and know I love you. A

I wonder how your company manages to stay in business as long as they have. It very much sounds like a dysfunctional family. May you be an island of peace and serenity. Enjoy your lunch and the day. Love, A

I look at our house, as have you, and wonder if it is time to move. There have been a lot of memories that we would leave behind over the past thirty years. Lisa started high school, Kellie was starting grade 7 and Andrea and Natasha really didn't know any other place. A new place would need a dining room that could accommodate at least 10 people, and we would still need a good size kitchen. I wouldn't miss the swimming pool though, as it has become an extravagant expense since the kids moved out. Lots to think about. Love, A

I feel that you are always with me, no matter where I go. Having lived together so long, I guess we become a part of each other, so when we are apart for any length of time, it leaves a bit of a hole. That is why I am always happy to be around you and have you near me. Love, A

It will be nice to see Lisa and Tracy and the kids this weekend. In the meantime, before they come, have a nice day. The weather is supposed to be nice, and maybe even warm enough to take a walk at lunch. May the workday be finished before you look at the clock to realize it is over. Love, A

It has been a wonderful weekend; finally seeing all the kids and grandchildren in one place. I'm not sure what the drive home will be like, but be careful. Who would think that we get ten centimeters of snow on the third of April? Oh well, enjoy the day and I will see you at home this evening. Love, A.

I didn't get a chance to write a note yesterday, having left really early. I want you to know that what you did for Easter was amazing — entertaining and cooking for twenty-two people. In some ways that was the easy part. By the time I came home, the place was immaculate. You managed all this before leaving for work. Now I wish you much good health and to leave those cramps behind. Love, A

I never know what I am writing until I sit down and start. Sometimes I wonder beforehand and think how I can write something without getting stale and repeating myself. Then here I am, writing. I imagine you in so many different ways and every way I see you reminds me of what makes you so special. Love, A

I am glad to see you are on the mend. Hopefully it will continue in the fashion for the rest of today so that by the time you get home, you will be one hundred percent. You mean far too much to me for you to remain sick. Sickness is something we all experience from time to time. Most of the time it passes once our immune system kicks in. Love, A

I am really looking forward to spending a nice long weekend with you. The temperature there will be so warm. There will be no snow shovelling, and we may get some solitude in the forest. Looking to this "now" moment, I wish you a wonderful day with very little hassle. Enjoy your lunch and hopefully your book. You are loved more than all the brown grass blades in our yard. Love, A

Even though you had a rough evening with an inordinate amount of phone calls, I felt good just knowing you were in the house. Besides, we got to hold hands in the back seat of Andrea and Donny's car while looking at houses with them. The hand holding in the back seat reminded me of the teenage years. So, the weekend wasn't a total loss. We got to be teenagers again for a couple of hours. Love, A

Well Ashie, it was love at first sight and it will be love at last sight. I'm looking forward to a nice weekend in the wilderness with you. I am not sure if there will be enough snow to do some snowshoeing and we can certainly sit in front of a nice fireplace if nothing else.

What a wonderful weekend. Gourmet meals a hot tub on the balcony and most important, you. The trip through the park was also nice and most of the animals were still hibernating or just shy. Whenever you are with me, the trips always become special. That is why I am so grateful to have you in my life. Love, A

Sometimes you are so efficient with cleaning up. Case in point, you moved my egg timer into the kitchen but it is for the office as I use it as a meditation timer, something I don't do in the kitchen. I do understand how much you love me. It is the little things you do, such as hugging up to me at night, a small back rub when I least expect it, and sharing little things with me. I really enjoy spending time with you in such intimate ways. Love, A

Happy Anniversary, we have now been married 33 years and other than a couple of rough patches, it has been a very happy time we have spent together. I see no reason why our love cannot continue to grow. You are a very special person that I am happy to continue spending the rest of my life with. Love, A.

Thank you for always being supportive. The reason for wanting to do things for myself as much as possible is because I don't want you to be my personal servant. You are so giving that it would be easy to fall into a situation where suddenly I'm taking advantage of my back pain. Besides, I want to keep moving. I love you a whole bunch. A

I am sorry I kept you awake most of the night with my back pain. Hopefully you will have a better night's sleep tonight. Enjoy the day and your haircut this evening. Love, A

Hopefully this will be a wonderful weekend. I am looking forward to the back and leg pain finally abating and that we can do some fun things together. Of course, I don't need to be healthy to have a good time with you. Love, A

Thank you for your tremendous support over the weekend. Lower back pain is not pleasant. I can be stubborn at times, not wanting help, but you managed to have me take it easy for the most part. The pain seemed to come at the most unexpected times. Your gentle touch, your willingness to do those things I really appreciate you. May your doctor's visit have lots of good news. Love, A

Thank you for being the wonderful lady that you are. It seems that we will be getting some freezing rain, so be careful on your way home. I guess we should have gone to Cuba with Colm because the weather for the remainder of the week does not look promising. Love, A

Anniversary is over, Family Day is over and so is Valentine's Day. It has been a wonderful weekend. Just because those days are over, doesn't mean that we stop celebrating our love for each other. You see, we do not need special occasions to commemorate our love for each other; that is a daily practice. It was nice to spend time with our future in-laws as well. Love, A.

Winter could not have come at a worse time. All winter there has been no snow and now, the end of February it decides that because it is still winter, some snow should fall. And, just for fun, let's add some rain to the mix. All this would not be an issue it wasn't for my back to add to the aggravation. It has kept me out of the gym, and now left the driveway in a mess because I can't maneuver the snow blower. Be careful out there. Enjoy lunch and church this evening. Love, PC

It seems winter will finally arrive on the first day of March. There will be twenty centimeters of snow between this afternoon and tomorrow. Please be careful on the drive home. You should know that Burton Manor may decide to cancel — which is not a bad thing. If you do go, be careful of driving. I love you madly and more than all the snowflakes that follow. A.

Thank you for always supporting me. Your support is greatly appreciated. May your day be bright on such a gloomy day. It seems like Mother Nature is getting a bit senile. It is March and the precipitation is as though it is April with all its showers. Enjoy the day and I will see you this evening. Don't forget I am having dinner with Jen this evening. Love, A

I hope you are feeling much better today and that work will not be too taxing for you. You made quite a nice recovery from yesterday. That also had a lot to do with staying in bed and getting the rest you needed. The fact you were able to heal quicker than some that are felled by this kind of illness for days, is a testament to the healthy lifestyle you live. Love, A

I am so happy that you have bounced back so quickly with your health. Although not one hundred percent yet, you are well on your way. There is nothing worse than being sick. It makes you uncomfortable and sort of helpless because the illness has drained you of energy as well. Love, FP

Every day, I find some way to say, "I love you". I don't know if you ever get tired of me saying so, as I am sure you know how I feel about you. It is a feeling inside me that does not go away and needs to be expressed. I wish you have a peaceful day and enjoy your lunch. Love, A

At times it is hard to explain how much I care for you. My feelings for you are kind of a longing for you, just as it was after our first "date". I feel this way even though we have been with each other for 35 years. Who says love gets stale? Love, A

Occasionally we have to change the notes up a bit because they can be repetitive and become uninteresting. While I won't be a philosopher in writing these notes, perhaps I will switch things around a bit and talk about the weather, birds, neighbours, who knows what? Enjoy the day and evening out. I love you madly, A.

There are time like today where I have a somewhat light schedule and think how wonderful it would be to just spend time together — like the whole day. We could just pretend to be away at a resort. We could take a little road trip and have dinner at some small roadside restaurant that makes fabulous food. Then we could come home early enough to kick back and relax. Love, A

Since we are coming upon the weekend it is entering a period of relaxation. It seems there will be no such opportunity for you, as you will be with your uncle and cousin Saturday morning, as they will be leaving for England to visit family. Sunday it is to try and find a dress for Natasha and her wedding entourage. So try to relax through your lunch and enjoy the day. Love, A.

I love you and am looking forward to spending some time with you on the weekend. Have a great day and enjoy the evening.

Listening to stories about your work environment is very frustrating. It seems that everyone sees what needs to be done except those who can actually do something about it. It is kind of amusing though, to see that you are the focal point for others to complain to as though you were in a position to fix all the ills of the company. They don't seem to understand that you are in the same boat as everyone else. Sit back, relax and enjoy lunch. Love, A

Sometimes it is almost not worth washing your car. Well at least it looked good for a couple of days before the snow and slush decided to un-wash the car. Funny, we tell the kids not to play in the mud, but then our cars play in it; yet it is cheaper to wash the kids than to wash the car. Oh well, have a nice day and know that I love you. Enjoy dinner this evening. Love, A

What a lovely weekend. We had a wonderful evening on Saturday. I liked the restaurant and the ambiance of Fonzorelli's, and the food was really good as well. Yesterday we had the siblings over. It is always nice to see them. While dinner discussions were quite lively, we then settled in to watch the Oscars. All this to say I really love you. A.

Have a great day and enjoy. Hopefully your lunch will be tasty. I used Lisa's spices. I look forward to having you home this evening. I make a mental note to see you as I saw you the first time I laid eyes on you. It reminds me of the beautiful woman I first met all those years ago. I am constantly reminded why we married. Your beauty both inner and outer, is what attracted me to you. It is the love of your character, personality, compassion for others that I really fell in love with. You have taught me so much about love and how to express that with other people. I will always be grateful for all that you have done for me. That's why I look forward to seeing you each evening. It is the anticipation of being able to spend a lovely evening with my best friend. I am so grateful that I got to be your husband, instead of just admiring you from afar. Love, A

This ends the notes to the lunch bag as the place that Norma worked at closed down. Instead of looking for other work, she has decided to retire.

Forever

Printed in the United States
By Bookmasters